THE MODERN RANSOMWARE FILES

UNDERSTANDING THE RANSOMWARE THREAT How Cybercriminals Attack and What You Can Do About It

Based on the Research of

DR. AHMED TAWER

Authornest publishing

Understanding the Ransomware Threat

The Ransomware Files, Book One

Based on doctoral research conducted at the University of the Cumberlands

Published by Logic Minds Publishing

First Edition

Printed in the United States of America

For the defenders—

the security professionals who work tirelessly

to protect our digital world.

PREFACE

This book exists because ransomware has become one of the defining cybersecurity challenges of our time.

Every week brings news of another attack. Hospitals locked out of patient records. Businesses paralyzed for days or weeks. City governments forced to revert to paper and pen. Schools unable to function. The damage extends far beyond the ransom payments themselves—though those payments now routinely reach into the millions.

Yet most of what business leaders and IT professionals know about ransomware comes from headlines and vendor marketing. They hear about attacks but rarely understand how they actually work, why they succeed so often, or what genuinely protects against them.

This book aims to change that.

The content you'll find here is based on doctoral research conducted at the University of the Cumberlands, examining the lived experiences of seventeen data security experts who deal with ransomware threats as part of their daily work. These aren't theorists or commentators—they're practitioners who have responded to real attacks, implemented real defenses, and learned hard lessons about what works and what doesn't.

Their insights form the backbone of this book.

The original research followed rigorous academic methodology, but this book translates those findings into accessible language for business leaders and IT professionals who need practical understanding, not academic jargon. Where the dissertation analyzed themes and subthemes, this book tells the story of ransomware—how it evolved, how it attacks, and how organizations can defend themselves.

This is the first volume in a planned three-book series derived from the research. It focuses on understanding the threat—what ransomware is, how attacks work, and why they keep succeeding. Subsequent volumes will address defense strategies and organizational response in greater depth.

My hope is that this book helps you understand ransomware well enough to take it seriously—and practically enough to do something about it.

The threat is real. But so are the defenses.

— Dr. Ahmed Tawer January 2025

INTRODUCTION

Imagine walking into your office on a Monday morning. You turn on your computer. Instead of your familiar desktop, you see a red screen with a countdown timer and a message:

"Your files have been encrypted. You have 72 hours to pay $500,000 in Bitcoin. If you don't pay, your data will be deleted — and published online."

Your customer records. Your financial data. Years of work. All locked. All held hostage.

This isn't a movie scene. This happens to businesses every single day.

Why This Book?

Ransomware attacks have exploded. What started as a strange experiment on floppy disks in 1989 has become a multi-billion dollar criminal industry. Hospitals have been shut down. Schools have lost student records. Companies have gone bankrupt.

And it's getting worse.

The attackers are getting smarter. They're not just locking your files anymore — they're stealing your data first. They threaten to publish your secrets if you don't pay. They target backups. They attack on weekends when no one is watching.

Most business leaders and IT managers know ransomware is a threat. But few truly understand how it works, how attackers get in, or why attacks keep growing.

This book changes that.

What You'll Learn

This book is based on research with 17 data security experts who deal with ransomware attacks every day. These are the people on the front lines — the ones who investigate breaches, respond to attacks, and help companies recover.

Their insights reveal:

- How ransomware evolved from a $189 scam to million-dollar extortion schemes
- The most common ways attackers get into your systems
- The security holes they exploit again and again
- Why ransomware attacks are growing faster than ever

Understanding the threat is the first step to fighting it.

Who This Book Is For

This book is for:

- **Business leaders** who need to understand what they're up against
- **IT managers** who want to see the big picture, not just technical details
- **Anyone** who wants to understand why ransomware has become such a massive problem

You don't need to be a cybersecurity expert to read this book. We've taken complex technical concepts and explained them in plain language. No jargon. No assumptions. Just clear explanations of how ransomware really works.

How This Book Is Organized

This book has four parts:

Part I: The Evolution of Ransomware How did we get here? We trace ransomware from its strange beginnings in 1989 to the sophisticated attacks of today.

Part II: How Attackers Get In The front doors criminals use to enter your systems — phishing emails, malicious websites, and weak remote access.

Part III: Security Holes Attackers Exploit The technical vulnerabilities that make attacks possible — from zero-day flaws to fileless malware that leaves no trace.

Part IV: Why Attacks Keep Growing The forces driving the ransomware explosion — cryptocurrency, criminal business models, and more.

A Note About the Research

The insights in this book come from a doctoral research study conducted in 2025. The study interviewed 17 data security experts with five to 20 years of experience dealing with ransomware threats. Their real-world experiences and observations form the foundation of what you'll read.

When you see expert quotes throughout the book, these come directly from those interviews. We've kept their words but removed identifying details to protect their privacy.

The Threat Is Real — But So Is Hope

Ransomware is scary. But knowledge is power.

The more you understand about how these attacks work, the better you can protect yourself, your company, and your people. The attackers count on confusion and fear. This book gives you clarity.

Let's begin.

Table of Contents

PART I

THE EVOLUTION OF RANSOMWARE

CHAPTER 1
HOW IT ALL STARTED

In 1989, something strange happened at an international AIDS research conference. Attendees received floppy disks in the mail — 20,000 of them. The disks claimed to contain helpful information about AIDS research. But they contained something else entirely.

The disks were sent by Dr. Joseph Popp, a World Health Organization consultant and AIDS researcher. When people inserted the disk into their computers, the software quietly counted how many times the computer was turned on. After 90 reboots, the program locked the computer and displayed a message demanding payment.

The ransom? $189, sent to a physical mailing address in Panama.

This was the AIDS Trojan — the world's first ransomware attack.

A Simple But Clever Trick

By today's standards, the AIDS Trojan was simple. It didn't use fancy encryption. It didn't spread across networks. It came on a floppy disk through regular mail.

But the basic idea was the same as modern ransomware:

1. Get into someone's computer
2. Lock them out of their files
3. Demand money to give access back

Dr. Popp was eventually caught. He claimed the money was meant for AIDS research. But his creation planted a seed a blueprint that cybercriminals would later turn into a billion-dollar criminal industry.

The Quiet Years

After the AIDS Trojan, ransomware went quiet for nearly two decades. Why?

Payment was the problem. In 1989, there was no easy way to collect ransom anonymously. Victims had to mail checks or money orders to physical addresses. This made it easy for law enforcement to track down criminals.

Computers weren't connected. The internet was barely used by regular people. Without email or websites, there was no way to spread malware quickly to thousands of victims.

Security wasn't a concern. Most people didn't even think about computer security. There was no antivirus software industry. No cybersecurity experts. No reason to worry about digital threats.

So ransomware stayed in the shadows. Waiting.

What Changed Everything

Two things happened that brought ransomware roaring back:

The internet connected everyone. By the 2000s, millions of people were online. Email became the main way people communicated. Websites popped up everywhere. Suddenly, criminals could reach thousands of victims with a single click.

Cryptocurrency made payment anonymous. When Bitcoin launched in 2009, it changed the game completely. Now criminals could demand payment without revealing their identity. No bank accounts. No mailing addresses. Just anonymous digital wallets that were nearly impossible to trace.

These two changes turned ransomware from a curiosity into a crisis.

The Lessons from 1989

Looking back at the AIDS Trojan, we can see patterns that still apply today:

Social engineering works. Dr. Popp didn't hack into computers. He tricked people into inserting his disk by making it look helpful and legitimate. Modern attackers do the same thing with phishing emails.

Criminals target what matters. Popp targeted AIDS researchers — people who desperately needed their data. Today's attackers target hospitals, schools, and businesses that can't afford to lose access to their systems.

Simple attacks can cause big damage. The AIDS Trojan was basic, but it still locked people out of their computers. You don't need sophisticated technology to cause serious harm.

What Comes Next

The AIDS Trojan was just the beginning. In the next chapter, we'll see how ransomware evolved from that simple floppy disk into the sophisticated threat it is today — complete with double extortion, data theft, and criminal organizations that operate like businesses.

The story of ransomware is a story of criminals getting smarter, faster, and more dangerous. Understanding where it started helps us understand where it's going.

Key Takeaways

- The first ransomware appeared in 1989, spread via floppy disks
- Dr. Joseph Popp demanded $189 sent to a physical address
- Ransomware stayed quiet for years because payment was hard to collect anonymously
- The internet and cryptocurrency changed everything
- The basic tactics from 1989 — tricking people and locking their data — still work today

CHAPTER 2
THE RISE OF MODERN RANSOMWARE

The AIDS Trojan was just a preview. When ransomware came back, it came back with a vengeance.

Today's ransomware doesn't just lock your screen. It encrypts every file you have. It steals your data before encrypting it. And it threatens to publish your secrets if you don't pay.

This chapter tells the story of how ransomware evolved from a simple lock on your screen to the sophisticated threat it is today.

Two Types of Ransomware

Modern ransomware comes in two main flavors:

Locker Ransomware

Locker ransomware is the simpler type. It locks you out of your computer completely. When you turn on your device, instead of your normal desktop, you see a full-screen message demanding payment. You can't access anything — not your files, not your programs, nothing.

The screen usually shows a countdown timer. Pay before time runs out, or lose everything.

Locker ransomware doesn't actually encrypt your files. Your data is still there, untouched. The ransomware just blocks you from reaching it. This means tech experts can sometimes remove the lock without paying.

Examples include Reveton and WinLocker.

Crypto Ransomware

Crypto ransomware is far more dangerous. It doesn't just lock your screen — it encrypts your actual files. Every document, photo, spreadsheet, and database gets scrambled with complex encryption. Without the decryption key, your files are useless garbage.

As one security expert explained:

"Crypto ransomware encrypts files on a device and prevents the victim from accessing the encrypted files unless they pay a ransom."

This is why crypto ransomware has become the weapon of choice for cybercriminals. Even if you remove the ransomware from your computer, your files stay encrypted. The only ways to recover are: pay the ransom, restore from backup, or lose everything.

The Infamous Attacks

Several crypto ransomware attacks made worldwide headlines:

WannaCry (2017)

WannaCry spread like wildfire across the globe in May 2017. In just one day, it infected over 200,000 computers in 150 countries. It hit hospitals, banks, and government agencies.

The UK's National Health Service was hit hard. Hospitals had to turn away patients. Surgeries were cancelled. Ambulances were diverted.

What made WannaCry so dangerous? It spread automatically from computer to computer without anyone clicking anything. Once it got into a network, it infected every vulnerable machine it could find.

Petya and NotPetya (2017)

Petya arrived shortly after WannaCry. But NotPetya — a variant that appeared a month later — was even more destructive.

NotPetya didn't just encrypt files. It destroyed them. Many victims who paid the ransom discovered they couldn't recover their data anyway. The encryption was designed to cause maximum damage, not to make money.

NotPetya caused over $10 billion in damage worldwide. Shipping giant Maersk lost $300 million. Pharmaceutical company Merck lost $870 million.

Locky (2016)

Locky spread through email attachments. Open the wrong Word document, and your files were encrypted within minutes.

At its peak, Locky was infecting 90,000 computers per day.

GandCrab, Ryuk, and SamSam

After the famous 2017 attacks, ransomware kept evolving. GandCrab and Ryuk dominated 2018. SamSam targeted hospitals and city governments in 2019.

Each new variant learned from the ones before it. They got better at hiding. Better at spreading. Better at making money.

The Game Changer: Double Extortion

Then came the biggest shift in ransomware history: double extortion.

Here's how traditional ransomware worked:

1. Attackers encrypt your files
2. You pay ransom to get the decryption key
3. You restore your files

Simple. And businesses found a way around it — backups. If you had good backups, you could restore your files without paying.

Attackers noticed this. So they changed the game.

Now here's how double extortion works:

1. Attackers steal your sensitive data first
2. Then they encrypt your files
3. They demand ransom — and threaten to publish your stolen data if you don't pay

Even if you have perfect backups, you still face a nightmare. Your customer data, financial records, trade secrets — all of it could be published online or sold to competitors.

One expert described it this way:

"Some attacks are designed for double extortion purposes, where the attackers exfiltrate a victim's sensitive data in addition to encrypting it. These tactics give threat actors additional leverage to put pressure on victims to pay a ransom."

This tactic has become standard. As another expert noted:

"Double extortion is becoming a standard part of the ransomware attack evolution."

Why Backups Aren't Enough Anymore

For years, the advice was simple: keep good backups, and you can recover from ransomware without paying.

That advice is now incomplete.

With double extortion, attackers hold two things hostage: your files AND your reputation. Backups can restore your files. But backups can't un-steal your data.

One security expert explained:

"Even if business organizations have backups, the threat of data leakage to the public can compel victims to pay the ransom to avoid erosion of customer trust due to reputational damage."

And attackers have gotten smarter about backups too. Modern ransomware often:

- Searches for and encrypts backup files
- Deletes Windows shadow copies (automatic backup snapshots)
- Attacks cloud storage that syncs with infected computers

As one expert warned:

"Any changes made to a file and saved on a shared solution such as Dropbox or OneDrive may also sync to the cloud environment, allowing ransomware-infected files residing on the local network to sync to the cloud."

Backups are still essential. But they're no longer a complete solution.

The Human Cost

Ransomware doesn't just damage computers. It damages people.

The research revealed something often overlooked: the psychological toll on those who respond to attacks.

One expert shared:

"A ransomware attack involving double extortion is not easy to deal with. Some IT staff members often suffer from severe sleep deprivation and stay awake for longer hours to resolve the ransomware situation."

Another added:

"Senior management typically focuses on keeping the business running and is more concerned about losing customer trust and facing reputational damage. But IT staff deal with the attackers' harassment tactics directly."

Behind every ransomware statistic are real people stressed, exhausted, and under enormous pressure.

What Comes Next

Ransomware has evolved from simple screen locks to sophisticated extortion operations. The attackers have moved from targeting individuals to targeting businesses, hospitals, and critical infrastructure.

But understanding the types of ransomware is only part of the picture. In the next chapter, we'll look at something even more alarming: how anyone — even people with no technical skills — can now launch ransomware attacks thanks to the rise of Ransomware-as-a-Service.

Key Takeaways

- Locker ransomware blocks access to your device; crypto ransomware encrypts your files
- Famous attacks like WannaCry, Petya, and Locky caused billions in damage
- Double extortion changed everything — attackers now steal data before encrypting it
- Backups alone are no longer enough protection
- Ransomware attacks cause significant psychological stress on those who respond

CHAPTER 3
RANSOMWARE-AS-A-SERVICE

In the past, launching a ransomware attack required serious technical skills. You needed to know how to write malicious code, build encryption systems, and set up payment infrastructure.

Not anymore.

Today, anyone can launch a ransomware attack. No coding required. No technical expertise needed. All you need is money and bad intentions.

Welcome to Ransomware-as-a-Service.

The Criminal Franchise Model

Think of RaaS like a fast-food franchise — but for cybercrime.

In a normal franchise, a company like McDonald's develops the recipes, builds the brand, and creates the operating systems. Franchisees pay to use all of that and run their own locations.

RaaS works the same way:

Developers create the ransomware. They write the code, build the encryption, set up payment systems, and handle customer support. Yes, customer support — criminals helping victims figure out how to pay.

Affiliates pay to use the ransomware. They don't need to know how it works. They just need to get it onto victims' computers.

When a victim pays, the money gets split. Developers might take 20-30%. Affiliates keep the rest.

As one security expert explained:

"In most cases, cybercriminals rent or purchase the entire ransomware payload from RaaS providers, who provide complete customer support and other technical services to affiliates usually via the dark web."

No Coding Skills Required

This is the most alarming part: RaaS has removed the technical barrier completely.

One expert put it bluntly:

"Ransomware-as-a-Service model has spiked the global spread of ransomware. This is because coding was a requirement for all successful cyberattacks in the past. But with the technical services introduced via the RaaS model, this technical prerequisite was completely offset."

Another expert described it this way:

"The advent of the ransomware-as-a-service model has shifted cybercriminals' strategy to rent or purchase ransomware packages to anyone, even to those with little or no programming skills, to launch ransomware attacks."

Think about what this means. Someone with no technical background can now:

- Subscribe to a RaaS platform
- Download a ready-to-use ransomware package
- Get step-by-step instructions

- Launch attacks on businesses
- Collect ransom payments

The RaaS platforms even look like legitimate businesses. They have websites. Marketing videos. Twitter accounts. Tutorial videos on YouTube.

As one expert observed:

"RaaS operators run marketing campaigns and have websites that look exactly like legitimate business websites. They have videos and are active on Twitter to make huge money by selling sophisticated exploit kits."

How the Dark Web Marketplace Works

RaaS operates primarily on the dark web — the hidden part of the internet that requires special software to access.

Here's how a typical RaaS operation works:

Step 1: Developers Build the Product

Skilled programmers create sophisticated ransomware. They test it. They update it. They make sure it can evade security software.

Step 2: Marketing and Sales

Developers advertise their RaaS products on dark web forums. They offer different subscription packages — just like Netflix or Spotify, but for crime.

Step 3: Affiliates Subscribe

Would-be attackers browse the marketplace and choose a RaaS product. They pay a subscription fee or agree to share a percentage of future ransoms.

Step 4: Training and Support

Affiliates receive the ransomware package along with instructions. Many RaaS providers offer ongoing technical support. Having trouble getting the ransomware to work? They'll help you troubleshoot.

Step 5: Launch Attacks

Affiliates use phishing emails, malicious websites, or other methods to infect victims. When a victim pays, the money is automatically split between developer and affiliate.

One expert described the support structure:

"RaaS permits less technically savvy cyber actors to enter the cybercriminals' ecosystem, learn the basics of ransomware attacks on YouTube tutorials, or obtain help from ransomware syndicates, which charge a fee to set them up to run ransomware attacks in exchange for a portion of the money."

Famous RaaS Operations

Several RaaS operations have become notorious:

REvil

REvil was one of the most sophisticated RaaS operations. They didn't just encrypt files — they stole data first and threatened to publish it. Their attacks hit major companies and demanded ransoms in the millions.

Conti

Conti operated like a corporation. They had HR departments, training programs, and performance bonuses. They recruited affiliates through job postings on the dark web.

LockBit

LockBit advertised speed as their selling point. Their ransomware could encrypt a corporate network faster than competitors making it harder for security teams to stop.

Why RaaS Changed Everything

RaaS transformed ransomware from a technical challenge into a business opportunity. Here's why it matters:

More Attackers

Before RaaS, only skilled programmers could launch ransomware attacks. Now, anyone with criminal intent can participate. This has dramatically increased the number of attacks.

Better Quality

RaaS developers compete for affiliates. This drives them to create more sophisticated ransomware — better encryption, better evasion, better results.

Harder to Catch

When attacks were launched by the developers themselves, law enforcement could sometimes trace them. Now, the people launching attacks aren't the people who made the ransomware. Even if you catch an affiliate, the developers continue operating.

As one expert noted:

"The shift of cybercriminals towards the RaaS business model was a significant development, indicating that identifying ransomware developers and prosecuting them across jurisdictional boundaries is becoming more challenging."

Specialization

RaaS allows criminals to specialize. Some focus on writing code. Some focus on finding victims. Some focus on laundering money. This division of labor makes the whole operation more effective.

The Numbers Don't Lie

The research revealed just how much RaaS has fueled the ransomware explosion:

"The RaaS business model has made ransomware actors more accessible and profitable than ever before, as ransomware actors with little programming skills can now launch and execute successful ransomware attacks on their targeted business organizations."

And:

"RaaS helps lower the barrier to entry for cybercriminals and expands their attack surface, making it more difficult for business organizations to combat ransomware threats effectively."

The bottom line: RaaS has industrialized cybercrime.

What Makes RaaS So Dangerous

The experts identified several factors that make RaaS particularly threatening:

Mutual Benefit

Both developers and affiliates profit. Developers make money without taking the risk of launching attacks. Affiliates get access to sophisticated tools they couldn't build themselves. This creates a stable, profitable ecosystem.

Low Risk for Developers

RaaS developers can run their operations from countries with weak cybercrime laws. They never directly attack anyone — their affiliates do. This makes them very hard to prosecute.

Continuous Improvement

Like legitimate software companies, RaaS developers constantly update their products. They patch bugs. They add features. They respond to security improvements with their own improvements.

Scale

A single RaaS operation can have hundreds of affiliates, all launching attacks simultaneously. This creates an overwhelming volume of attacks that security teams struggle to address.

The Profit Motive

At its core, RaaS is about money. One expert described it simply:

"Making money is the primary reason behind the recent surge in ransomware attacks against various business organizations;

because it is the easiest way for cyber actors to make money by subscribing for RaaS service, while sitting behind a keyboard."

Another put it more vividly:

"Imagine if people were able to steal data, walk away, and threaten the company to pay us a huge ransom without getting caught. This is the way cybercriminals get paid on the dark web."

What Comes Next

RaaS has fundamentally changed the ransomware landscape. Attacks that once required sophisticated hackers can now be launched by anyone.

But attackers still need a way in. In Part II, we'll explore exactly how they get into your systems — through phishing emails, malicious websites, and weak remote access.

Understanding these entry points is the first step to blocking them.

Key Takeaways

- RaaS lets anyone launch ransomware attacks — no coding skills needed
- It works like a franchise: developers create the tools, affiliates launch the attacks
- RaaS operations include customer support, tutorials, and marketing — just like legitimate businesses
- The model has dramatically increased the number and sophistication of attacks

- RaaS makes attackers harder to catch because developers and attackers are different people
- The primary motivation is profit — RaaS is a business

PART II
HOW ATTACKERS GET IN

CHAPTER 4
PHISHING — THE EMAIL TRAP

Every major ransomware attack starts somewhere. And more often than not, it starts with an email.

Phishing remains the number one way attackers get into organizations. Despite years of warnings, training programs, and spam filters, it still works. Why? Because attackers have gotten incredibly good at it.

This chapter reveals how modern phishing attacks work — and why they're harder to stop than ever.

What Is Phishing?

Phishing is simple in concept: trick someone into doing something they shouldn't.

That might mean:

- Clicking a malicious link
- Opening an infected attachment
- Entering login credentials on a fake website
- Transferring money to a fraudulent account

The name comes from "fishing" — attackers cast out bait and wait for someone to bite.

The Evolution of Phishing

Phishing has come a long way from the obvious scam emails of the past.

Old-School Phishing

Remember those emails from Nigerian princes? Poor grammar. Obvious lies. Easy to spot.

Those still exist, but they're not the real threat anymore.

Modern Phishing

Today's phishing emails look legitimate. They use correct grammar. They reference real events. They appear to come from people you know.

As one security expert observed:

"Phishing attacks have become more sophisticated and challenging to detect or prevent. Attackers use advanced social engineering techniques to create tailored and convincing messages that appear to come from a legitimate or trusted source."

The difference is night and day.

Phishing Kits: Attack in a Box

Here's what's changed the game: phishing kits.

Just like Ransomware-as-a-Service lowered the barrier for launching ransomware, phishing kits have made phishing attacks available to anyone.

A phishing kit includes:

- Ready-made email templates
- Fake website pages that look identical to real ones
- Scripts that capture login credentials

- Instructions for launching attacks

One expert explained:

"Phishing exploit kits are more dangerous and worrisome for businesses because they remove the barrier to entry for cybercriminal activity by requiring minimal technical skills to conduct a successful phishing campaign against targeted victims."

Another added:

"Phishing kits provide attackers with ready-made templates and scripts to create and execute malicious attacks against targeted business organizations."

These kits are sold on the dark web. They're constantly updated. And they work.

Spear Phishing: The Targeted Attack

Generic phishing casts a wide net. Spear phishing uses a sniper rifle.

In spear phishing, attackers research their targets. They learn:

- Who you work with
- What projects you're working on
- Who your boss is
- What software you use

Then they craft a personalized email that looks completely legitimate.

One expert shared a real example:

"A fraudulent email targeting a company's executive, including the CEO, is among the top phishing attacks because it is the most lucrative. Many times, I noticed that attackers often follow the path of those who manage the company's money or control valuable assets."

This is why executives are prime targets. One successful spear phishing email to a CFO can result in millions of dollars stolen.

Real Attack Stories

The security experts shared real incidents they've dealt with:

The Fake Invoice

"In December 2022, one of our employees received a fake invoice demanding a fraudulent purchase order. Unfortunately, he opened an email attachment that unleashed the malicious code on the machine. After remediation, a network database server was infected with the same ransomware variant three months later."

The Microsoft Teams Trick

"During the fake phone call, the ransomware actor instructed an employee in our company to allow a remote screen-control session through Microsoft Teams. Then, through this remote-control session, the attacker was able to open a command shell, drop malicious files, execute ransomware, and take control of Microsoft Office 365 login credentials."

The Repeat Offender

Even after fixing a problem, the same attack can come back:

"Modern cyber actors edit image files by stretching it, changing its color, and compressing it into a ZIP file format. This is one of the reasons users continue receiving the same phishing email, even after remediating the system and blocking the same email several times."

Why Email Filters Aren't Enough

You might think: "We have email filters. We're protected."

The experts disagree.

"Email filters usually catch random phishing attacks, but spear phishing attacks using phishing kits are more sophisticated and can avoid detection by email filters."

Another expert explained why:

"Email spam filters often fail to prevent Advanced Persistent Threats such as fileless ransomware or zero-day vulnerability attacks."

And:

"Sometimes, a phishing email may contain a PDF file or Word document that exhibits no malicious behavior and appears normal; however, when activated, it triggers a ransomware infection."

Attackers know how filters work. They design their attacks to get through.

Hidden Dangers: Password-Protected Files

One newer tactic: password-protected attachments.

Here's how it works:

1. Attacker sends an email with a password-protected ZIP file
2. The email includes the password
3. Email filters can't scan inside password-protected files
4. Victim opens the file, enters the password, and releases the malware

The research found:

"Ransomware actors use password-protected email attachments that contain malicious payloads. By employing password-protected files, attackers can bypass the initial security checks by obscuring the harmful payload within the password-protected file."

It's clever. And it works.

Images That Attack

Another technique: hiding malicious code inside images.

"A malicious code embedded within image-based phishing emails is difficult to prevent or detect using a human eye."

Attackers can embed code in what looks like an innocent photo or company logo. When opened, the code executes.

"Nowadays, cybercriminals easily alter an image to embed malicious code or hide it in a legitimate file format such as Word documents, PDF, ZIP files, or executable files."

This technique is called steganography — hiding data inside other data.

Beyond Email: SMS and Social Media

Phishing isn't limited to email anymore.

SMS Phishing (Smishing)

Attackers now send text messages with malicious links. One expert noted:

"Cybercriminals shifted their tactics into SMS messaging by sending fraudulent text messages to trick potential users into revealing sensitive personal information or clicking malicious links."

Social Media Attacks

Platforms like Telegram are being used to launch attacks:

"Attackers automate the delivery of phishing kits using messaging services such as Telegram and save the stolen information in a text file format and then transfer it in the form of small chunks of data to avoid detection."

The lesson: any communication channel can be a phishing vector.

Microsoft Office 365: A Growing Target

The experts identified a concerning trend: attacks targeting Microsoft Office 365.

"Cyber actors targeting Microsoft Office 365 is gaining traction among cybercriminals, which creates a challenge against Microsoft Office 365 business email, because often system administrators use their login credentials across different Microsoft Office 365 components, including OneDrive, SharePoint, and Dropbox."

Why this matters: if attackers get your Office 365 credentials, they can access:

- Your email
- Your cloud files
- Your shared documents
- Everything synced to your account

And infected files can sync to the cloud automatically:

"Files stored on a local network may synchronize with those stored on the cloud infrastructure."

One breach can spread everywhere.

AI-Powered Phishing

The future of phishing is even more concerning. Attackers are using artificial intelligence to create better attacks.

"With AI-powered ransomware, attackers can create more tailored and creative emails that prompt victims to click on a link, triggering autonomous downloads of malicious code onto their machines or devices."

And:

"With AI, cyber actors can create more personalized and authentic-looking phishing emails that are harder to detect."

Even deepfakes are being used:

"Cyber actors can leverage AI-empowered tools to create fake videos that mimic marketing departments and send them to recipients via email, prompting victims to respond to a special offer or register for a webinar, which may lead to a ransomware attack."

The Human Factor

At its core, phishing exploits people — not technology.

"Nearly all the top phishing attacks occurred due to a lack of basic security training and policies. A typical spam email may trick victims by using phrases like 'Click here for a prize' or 'Important update about your security clearance.'"

This is why training matters:

"Training employees to simulate phishing attacks and to understand, recognize, and report phishing attempts is the best option to keep data safe from the prying eyes of cybercriminals."

But training must include everyone — especially leadership:

"Top management should be included in cybersecurity training programs even if they feel that it is not an effective use of their time."

Attackers target the people with the most access and authority. Those are exactly the people who need training most.

What Comes Next

Phishing emails are the most common entry point — but they're not the only one.

In the next chapter, we'll look at another major attack vector: malicious websites. Attackers don't always wait for you to click a link in an email. Sometimes, they compromise websites you already trust.

Key Takeaways

- Phishing remains the #1 way attackers get into organizations
- Phishing kits have made sophisticated attacks available to anyone
- Spear phishing targets specific individuals with personalized attacks
- Email filters catch basic attacks but miss sophisticated ones
- Password-protected files and hidden code in images bypass security
- Attacks now come through SMS and social media, not just email
- Microsoft Office 365 is a growing target
- AI is making phishing emails more convincing
- Training everyone — including executives — is essential

CHAPTER 5
MALICIOUS WEBSITES AND DOWNLOADS

You don't always have to click a link in an email to get infected. Sometimes, just visiting a website is enough.

Attackers have turned the web itself into a weapon. They create fake sites. They inject malicious code into legitimate ones. They buy ads that deliver malware. And in some cases, they can infect your computer without you clicking anything at all.

This chapter reveals how attackers use the web to get into your systems.

Fake Websites: The Digital Impersonators

Attackers create fake websites that look identical to real ones. Banks. Software companies. Government agencies. If you're not paying close attention, you can't tell the difference.

One expert explained:

"Cybercriminals create fake websites to lure visitors to provide sensitive information or purchase nonexistent products. These fake websites are malicious Internet sites that exploit the anonymity of the Internet to mask their identity with the intention of luring users into fraud or malicious attacks."

These sites serve multiple purposes:

- Steal login credentials
- Capture credit card information

- Trick users into downloading malware
- Harvest personal data for future attacks

Another expert noted:

"Cyber actors use phishing kits to deploy fake webpages to send false security alerts to internet users, including offering giveaways or shopping gifts to create an impression of legitimacy."

The scale is staggering:

"Every day, week, and month, security teams block hundreds of fake pages. Some are short-lived, while others manage to infect our machines, scan the system, and attempt to steal data."

Exploit Kits: Automated Attack Machines

Exploit kits are packages of code designed to find and exploit vulnerabilities in your browser, plugins, or operating system. They're constantly updated to target the latest security holes.

One expert described how they work:

"Cyber actors use exploit kits that typically check for vulnerabilities in browser versions and plugins; even some bad actors test the exploit kits for each specific browser version or cloud-powered email."

What makes exploit kits so dangerous is their automation:

"Most of the exploit kits I analyzed are meant to work undetected by traditional security controls, such as antiviruses. They also covertly run automated scans for vulnerabilities without the knowledge of the victim who unwittingly browses the internet."

And they evolve constantly:

"Cybercriminals use exploit kits that are constantly evolving to adapt to new security patches and find new vulnerabilities to deliver malicious code without the victim's awareness. They can accomplish this through malicious advertisements, infected websites, or spoofed emails."

They're also designed to evade detection:

"The exploit kits were designed with evasion techniques to bypass detection, allowing the attackers to obfuscate their activities."

Drive-By Downloads: Infected Without Clicking

This is perhaps the most frightening attack vector: you can get infected just by visiting a website. No clicking required.

One expert explained:

"Drive-by download attacks can occur even if users only visit legitimate websites without clicking or downloading anything."

How is this possible?

"In drive-by download attacks, attackers exploit corrupted JavaScript or plugins to deliver their malicious code without the user being aware of the ongoing active attack. There are no signs that the target device is infected with ransomware or malware."

The experts emphasized how difficult these attacks are to stop:

"Drive-by download attacks are very challenging to prevent or detect because they work either by luring victims into clicking on malicious links and downloading ransomware code or by exploiting vulnerabilities in web browsers or software without user knowledge."

Crypto-ransomware — the type that encrypts your files — commonly spreads this way:

"Crypto-Ransomware is well-known for spreading through drive-by downloads, but now we see crypto ransomware code delivered also through social media, including web-based instant messaging applications."

Malvertising: Dangerous Ads

You might think you're safe if you stick to legitimate websites. You're not. Attackers buy advertising space on legitimate sites. These ads contain malicious code. When the ad loads, it can redirect you to malware or begin downloading it automatically.

One expert described it:

"Ransomware actors design malvertising ads to appear as legitimate or normal websites. However, when a victim clicks on it, they trigger malware downloads or are redirected to other malicious websites."

Another explained the process:

"Currently, ransomware actors simply rent exploit kits from the dark web to create tempting and tailored malvertising that tricks victims into believing the ad is legitimate or clicking on a fake website link containing malicious code to unknowingly download the ransomware payload into their systems."

The sophistication is alarming:

"Cyber actors create malvertising to deceive victims by providing sensitive personal information by filling out standard online forms, downloading documents, or signing up for mailing lists using their usernames and passwords."

Google Ads as Attack Vectors

Even Google search results aren't safe.

Attackers buy Google Ads that appear at the top of search results. These ads lead to fake websites that look exactly like the real thing.

One expert warned:

"Cyber actors leverage Google search engines to proliferate their malicious web advertisements, redirect victims to another fake webpages that look identical to a legitimate business webpage."

Think about it: you search for your bank's website. The first result is an ad — a malicious one. You click it, enter your credentials, and hand them directly to attackers.

Cross-Site Scripting (XSS): Turning Trusted Sites Against You

Attackers don't always need to create fake websites. Sometimes they inject malicious code into legitimate ones.

Cross-site scripting (XSS) attacks let attackers insert malicious scripts into trusted websites. When you visit, the malicious code runs in your browser.

One expert explained:

"Modern cyber actors use XSS to send a malicious script to a user to execute as a web application, as the browser has no way to recognize that it is not a trusted script."

Another described the impact:

"Cyber actors insert malicious code into JavaScript engines by stealing web session cookies to log in to the corresponding web application, gaining unauthorized access to the web server, performing login credential theft, or modifying website content."

This means even websites you trust completely can be used against you.

Why Traditional Defenses Fall Short

The experts were clear: traditional security tools struggle against these attacks.

"A single security solution is unlikely to detect or prevent ransomware exploit kit attacks because of the speed at which cybercriminals change and utilize new exploits to identify and exploit security vulnerabilities in software, browsers, plugins, and deliver malware or ransomware."

Even sandboxes — isolated environments designed to detect malware — have limitations:

"Cybercriminals learned that email sandboxes are resource-intensive and will not run indefinitely. Therefore, they instruct their malicious code to remain persistent until the sandbox finishes running on the system, and then they activate their malicious code."

Web filtering helps but isn't foolproof:

"Professional cyber actors with a good understanding of web filtering technology can bypass web filters using proxy websites and other techniques such as phishing kits, fake websites, drive-by downloads, and malvertising."

What Actually Works

The experts recommended a layered approach:

Web Filtering

"URL filtering solutions such as SIEM can reduce the risk of ransomware attacks by preventing employees from visiting malicious websites or downloading ransomware-infected files."

"Web filtering allows a business organization to promote safe browsing practices to ensure compliance with industry regulations by preventing employees from accessing risky sites that contain malicious content."

Behavioral Analysis

"In our company, we use web filtering software that provides behavioral analysis capabilities such as sandbox and SIEM tools to prevent zero-day exploits and identify obfuscation techniques used by the attacker."

But Most Importantly: Multiple Layers

"Defending ransomware exploit kits requires a multilayered security approach. Businesses are in dire need of applying multiple defensive layers that work together; therefore, if the attackers bypass one layer, the defenders still have additional protection layers. In short, there is no single solution, but rather a set of comprehensive detection and prevention strategies."

Training Remains Critical

Even with all the technology, human awareness matters:

"Education and training of employees about security must be an ongoing process, not an annual event."

Technical teams need specialized training:

"IT technical teams should receive ransomware-specific training programs more frequently that cover a range of in-depth cyberattack-related topics, including incident response and internal forensic investigation."

What Comes Next

Phishing emails and malicious websites are the most common attack vectors. But there's a third major entry point that's often overlooked: weak remote access.

In the next chapter, we'll explore how attackers exploit VPNs and Remote Desktop Protocol (RDP) — the tools that let employees work remotely — to break into corporate networks.

Key Takeaways

- Fake websites impersonate legitimate ones to steal credentials and deliver malware
- Exploit kits automatically scan for and exploit browser vulnerabilities

- Drive-by downloads can infect you just by visiting a website — no clicking required
- Malvertising places dangerous ads on legitimate websites
- Even Google Ads can be attack vectors
- Cross-site scripting turns trusted websites into attack platforms
- Traditional security tools struggle to keep up
- A multilayered defense approach is essential
- Continuous employee training remains critical

CHAPTER 6
THE REMOTE ACCESS PROBLEM

When COVID hit, millions of workers went home. Companies scrambled to set up remote access. VPNs and Remote Desktop Protocol became lifelines.

They also became attack vectors.

The same tools that let employees work from anywhere also let attackers in from anywhere. And many organizations still haven't fixed the vulnerabilities they created in that rush.

This chapter reveals how attackers exploit remote access — and why it's become one of their favorite ways in.

The Rise of Remote Access

Remote access isn't new. But its scale is.

Before 2020, remote access was mostly for IT administrators and traveling executives. Now it's for everyone. Every employee. Every device. Every day.

Two technologies dominate:

VPN (Virtual Private Network)

VPNs create encrypted tunnels between remote workers and company networks. They're supposed to be secure. The reality is more complicated.

RDP (Remote Desktop Protocol)

RDP is a Windows feature that lets you control one computer from another. It's incredibly useful — and incredibly dangerous when misconfigured.

The security experts ranked these threats clearly:

"Insecure Remote Desktop Protocol and VPN services ranked third on the list of cybersecurity threats, following email phishing and website infections."

Why Attackers Love RDP

RDP is everywhere in Windows environments. And it's often left wide open.

One expert explained:

"RDP is counted as one of the most common attack vectors favored by cybercriminals today, following phishing attacks and phishing fake websites."

The problems are systemic:

"Both VPNs and RDPs, by default, require manual patching. Thus, security teams are less likely to keep them updated."

And: "RDP ports are often left exposed to the Internet for extended periods owing to a lack of an automatic patching scheme, making RDP a valuable target for malicious attackers."

How RDP Attacks Work

Attackers have multiple ways to exploit RDP:

Brute Force Attacks

The most common method: try password after password until one works.

"Insecure RDP vulnerabilities allow attackers to brute-force their way into machines and change system configuration settings, serving a range of cybercriminals' interests such as moving from system to system, gaining access to login credentials, elevating privileges, and enumerating assets of interest to steal and transfer out of the network."

Default and Weak Passwords

Many RDP installations still use default passwords. Others use weak ones that are easy to guess.

"Cyber actors often use brute force to uncover and harvest default passwords and gain access to an organization's internal environment."

"Most cyber incidents occur due to RDP misconfiguration that leaves RDP insecure or running on default passwords, providing an easy way for attackers to infiltrate the system."

Stolen Credentials

Attackers buy RDP credentials on the dark web. Yes, there's a market for this.

"We noticed that cyber actors utilize login credentials obtained from the dark web to access insecure, Internet-facing RDP ports."

Research confirms that RDP credentials are actively traded on underground forums.

What Happens After They Get In

Once attackers have RDP access, the real damage begins.

Lateral Movement

"Cybercriminals extensively target insecure RDP to infect the victim's machine and move laterally to gain more sensitive information on the network, including accessing Windows built-in tools such as PowerShell to create scripts for data collection and exfiltration."

Disabling Security

This is particularly alarming:

"Once the attackers find the open RDP, they disable the system's antivirus to avoid detection. This is alarming for companies because even if the antivirus is updated, turning off the antivirus leaves the targeted victims' machines or network systems defenseless."

Privilege Escalation

"Threat actors escalate privileges and expand the scope of their attack on the infected network system using valid user accounts gained through RaaS brokers, purchased on the dark web, or social engineering."

Hiding Their Tracks

"The stealthiest ransomware actors often clear their footprints on the system, disable some features in the Windows environment such as system logs, delete traces after the attack, and hide the methods of malicious code delivery or execution."

VPN Vulnerabilities

VPNs are supposed to be secure. But they have their own problems.

One expert warned:

"I have noticed that cybercriminals often take advantage of vulnerabilities in how VPNs are configured to deliver and execute their ransomware code and gain unauthorized access to files they should not access."

The issues include:

Outdated Software

VPNs need regular updates. Many don't get them.

Configuration Flaws

Even good VPN software can be configured badly. Attackers look for these misconfigurations.

Fake VPNs

"Cybercriminals can trick users into downloading ransomware disguised as a VPN."

Think about that: the tool you're using for security might actually be malware.

The Pandemic Acceleration

The rush to remote work during COVID created massive security gaps.

"With the increased adoption of remote work environments, cybercriminals shifted to the RaaS business, which is a relatively low-risk business, providing an opportunity for attackers to make money easily by extorting victims."

Many organizations set up remote access quickly, without proper security. Those hasty configurations remain vulnerable today.

PowerShell: The Attacker's Favorite Tool

Once inside via RDP or VPN, attackers often turn to PowerShell — a powerful Windows scripting tool.

"PowerShell command continues to be the number one tool of choice for cybercriminals when executing malicious code and gaining initial access on network systems."

PowerShell is legitimate software. That's what makes it so dangerous — security tools often don't flag it as suspicious.

"Cyber actors rename their ransomware and abuse trusted applications like PowerShell to automate the download of additional tools and obfuscate their malicious activities."

The Challenge of Detection

Spotting attackers who use legitimate remote access tools is incredibly difficult.

"One of the challenging tasks I encountered while dealing with ransomware infection was spotting the attackers' lateral movement across the network."

Why? Because the activity looks normal. A user connecting via RDP. Someone running PowerShell scripts. These are things legitimate users do every day.

Attackers also work hard to blend in:

"Modern ransomware actors use persistence and various defense evasion techniques to maintain access to the target machine or network systems, evade detection, often using tools and sophisticated methods such as creating new accounts and obfuscating their activities once inside infected systems."

Public-Facing Applications

RDP and VPN aren't the only remote access targets. Attackers also exploit other public-facing applications.

"Ransomware actors often leverage known vulnerabilities in public-facing applications such as Microsoft Exchange Server and Microsoft Office 365 to launch zero-day attacks and gain access to the systems. Often, they exploit misconfigurations in these applications."

"Cybercriminals hunt for misconfigurations in Microsoft Exchange Server and Microsoft Office 365 applications to deliver their payload to a large pool of victims."

Any service exposed to the internet is a potential entry point.

The Cloud Connection

Remote access doesn't just threaten on-premise networks. It extends to cloud environments.

"If an infected device syncs with OneDrive, SharePoint, or other Microsoft Office 365 components or services, the ransomware can spread and encrypt files stored in the cloud environment."

And: "Ransomware attacks on local networks can synchronize with the cloud environment through file synchronization using Dropbox,

OneDrive, or SharePoint, thereby effectively spreading malicious payloads to other devices connected to cloud-based networks."

One breach can cascade across your entire infrastructure.

What Actually Protects You

The experts offered clear recommendations:

Turn Off What You Don't Need

"Security teams should proactively reduce the scope of RDP for attackers by disabling or limiting access to the RDP protocol and monitoring the network system for suspicious activities."

If you don't need RDP exposed to the internet, don't expose it.

Strong Passwords and Multi-Factor Authentication

This should be obvious, but it's still not universal. Weak passwords and lack of MFA remain primary attack enablers.

Regular Patching

"Security teams are less likely to keep RDP updated or patched promptly compared to other Windows applications and programs."

Make RDP and VPN patching a priority, not an afterthought.

Monitoring

Watch for suspicious activity: unusual login times, failed login attempts, connections from unexpected locations.

Policy and Permissions

"Establishing a cybersecurity policy and user permissions to manage access to RDP effectively cannot be overlooked."

Not everyone needs remote access. Limit it to those who truly require it.

This Ends Part II

We've now covered the three main ways attackers get in:

- Phishing emails (Chapter 4)
- Malicious websites (Chapter 5)
- Weak remote access (Chapter 6)

But getting in is just the beginning. In Part III, we'll explore what attackers do once inside — the security vulnerabilities they exploit to move through your network, steal your data, and deploy ransomware.

Key Takeaways

- RDP and VPN are among the top three attack vectors, after phishing and malicious websites
- RDP is often left exposed with default or weak passwords
- Attackers buy stolen RDP credentials on the dark web
- Once inside, attackers use legitimate tools like PowerShell to avoid detection
- VPNs have configuration vulnerabilities and can even be replaced with fake malware versions

- The COVID remote-work rush created security gaps that persist today
- Cloud environments can be infected through syncing with compromised local machines
- Disable unnecessary remote access, enforce strong authentication, and patch regularly

PART III
SECURITY HOLES ATTACKERS USE

CHAPTER 7
EXPLOITING WINDOWS FROM THE INSIDE

Getting into a network is only half the battle. Once attackers are inside, they need to stay hidden, move around, and avoid getting caught.

To do this, they turn Windows against itself.

Modern attackers don't rely on obvious malware that security software can easily spot. Instead, they exploit legitimate Windows features tools that are supposed to help the system run — to hide their activities, maintain access, and spread through networks.

This chapter reveals how attackers use your own operating system as a weapon.

The Problem with Trust

Windows is designed to trust certain things. Its own system files. Its own processes. Its own tools.

Attackers exploit this trust.

When malicious code runs as part of a legitimate Windows process, security software often doesn't flag it. It looks normal. It behaves like normal system activity. The attack hides in plain sight.

DLL Injection: The Invisible Attack

Dynamic Link Libraries (DLLs) are shared code libraries that Windows programs use. When you open your web browser, it loads dozens of DLLs. When you run Microsoft Office, it loads more. DLLs are everywhere in Windows — and attackers know how to abuse them.

What Is DLL Injection?

DLL injection is a technique where attackers insert malicious code into a legitimate running process. The malicious code rides along inside a trusted application.

One expert explained:

"DLL injection is stealthy because the attacker can exploit it, execute the malicious code, and run it in memory without human intervention."

The research found this is now common practice:

"Injecting malicious DLL code into memory has become a common practice among modern cyber actors designed to evade detection, maintain persistence, and escalate privileges."

Why It's So Dangerous

DLL injection works because security tools trust the applications being hijacked:

"DLL injections can allow attackers to evade security mechanisms because the application loading the DLL can be treated as a trusted application, where security solutions may not flag it as suspicious."

Once inside a trusted process, attackers can do almost anything:

"The impact of DLL injection depends on the attacker's intentions, where it can be used to infiltrate other systems on the network, spread malware to other devices, evade process-based defenses, elevate privileges, or steal login credentials."

Real Attack Examples

The experts shared what they've seen in the field:

"I have seen attackers load a malicious DLL file into memory and registry hives for weeks or months before launching their malicious activity, regardless of system reboots, credential changes, or shutdowns."

Another described credential theft:

"More often, I have seen that cyber actors inject a DLL into a web browser session cookie to trick victims into providing sensitive personal information such as usernames and login passwords, installing arbitrary code that triggers the downloading and execution of ransomware codes."

Disabling Security

Attackers use DLL injection to neutralize defenses:

"Ransomware operators are no longer satisfied with merely encrypting data and demanding ransom. Instead, they use the DLL injection technique to bypass or disable endpoint protection systems like antivirus before executing their malicious code."

Maintaining Persistence

Attackers don't just want to get in — they want to stay in. DLL injection helps them do that.

"DLL injection attacks are more challenging for defenders to detect or prevent promptly, as they enable attackers to encapsulate their malicious code within a legitimate application and execute it every time the application is launched."

They abuse Windows features like Task Scheduler:

"Attackers extensively exploit the Windows Task Scheduler service to automate the execution of malicious DLL code without user intervention, allowing them to maintain persistence and conduct reconnaissance and data gathering."

This persistence can last indefinitely:

"Maintaining persistence via the DLL injection technique is a critical challenge for security teams, allowing ransomware actors to establish persistence for extended periods, gain access to network resources, modify configuration settings, and propagate across the network to infect additional segments or nodes."

PowerShell: The Double-Edged Sword

PowerShell is one of the most powerful tools in Windows. IT administrators use it to automate tasks, manage systems, and run complex scripts.

Attackers use it for exactly the same reasons.

"PowerShell command continues to be the number one tool of choice for cybercriminals when executing malicious code and gaining initial access on network systems."

What makes PowerShell dangerous:

- It's pre-installed on every modern Windows system
- It has deep access to system functions
- It can download and execute code from the internet
- Security tools often don't flag it because it's a legitimate tool

"Cyber actors rename their ransomware and abuse trusted applications like PowerShell to automate the download of additional tools and obfuscate their malicious activities."

Attackers combine PowerShell with other techniques:

"Cybercriminals extensively target insecure RDP to infect the victim's machine and move laterally to gain more sensitive information on the network, including accessing Windows built-in tools such as PowerShell to create scripts for data collection and exfiltration."

Living Off the Land

Security researchers call this approach "living off the land" — using tools already present on the system instead of bringing in new malware.

The advantages for attackers are significant:

- No new files to detect
- Activities look like normal administration
- Tools are already trusted
- Harder to distinguish from legitimate use

"Modern ransomware actors exploit the Windows Scripting Interpreter of PowerShell and Command for malicious purposes, including lateral movement, fileless ransomware execution, and data exfiltration."

And:

"Ransomware actors can now leverage the Windows Task Scheduler service to automate tasks at specific times and evade security solutions during the Windows system startup."

Hiding Their Tracks

Sophisticated attackers don't just avoid detection — they actively cover their traces.

"The stealthiest ransomware actors often clear their footprints on the system, disable some features in the Windows environment such as system logs, delete traces after the attack, and hide the methods of malicious code delivery or execution."

They hide within normal Windows activities:

"Ransomware actors establish persistence on the targeted system or network for an extended time, allowing the attackers to hide their ransomware payloads behind standard Windows events, such as registry hives, memory processes, scheduled tasks, or DLL injection, making the incident response team's job more challenging."

The Detection Challenge

Detecting these attacks is extraordinarily difficult.

"The misuse of Windows native applications by cybercriminals confirmed that the detection of modern ransomware actors is more challenging to detect or prevent, as the activity appears to be a normal system process."

Traditional antivirus struggles:

"DLL ransomware is difficult to detect or prevent because it loads the Windows native DLL library by tricking the Windows Operating System into loading malicious code disguised as a legitimate DLL file. The stealthy execution of DLL as a Windows native application may allow cybercriminals to leave minimal traces and bypass traditional security solutions."

The research emphasized:

"Detecting DLL injection attacks is more challenging for defenders because running malicious code may enable attackers to gain higher levels of control over the system and evade detection."

What Defenders Can Do

The experts didn't leave organizations without hope. Several defensive measures can help:

Behavioral Analysis

Instead of looking for known malware signatures, look for unusual behavior:

- Programs accessing files they normally don't touch
- Unusual network connections
- Abnormal process relationships
- Unexpected PowerShell execution

Application Whitelisting

Control which applications can run and which DLLs they can load.

Endpoint Detection and Response (EDR)

Modern EDR solutions can detect suspicious behavior patterns, even from legitimate Windows tools.

Least Privilege

Limit what each user and application can do. If an attacker hijacks a limited account, the damage is limited too.

Regular Updates

"Installing security updates and patches as soon as they become available ensures that systems or networks are protected against the techniques employed by modern ransomware actors."

Multi-Layer Security

"Defenders should remain vigilant and constantly innovate to adapt multi-layer security approaches to detect and prevent the evasion techniques of modern ransomware threats."

What Comes Next

DLL injection and PowerShell abuse are just some of the techniques attackers use. In the next chapter, we'll explore zero-day attacks — exploits that target vulnerabilities no one knows exist yet.

These are among the most dangerous attacks because there's no patch to install, no signature to detect. The vulnerability is unknown until it's too late.

Key Takeaways

- Attackers use legitimate Windows features to hide malicious activities
- DLL injection allows malicious code to run inside trusted applications
- PowerShell is the #1 tool of choice for attackers due to its power and trusted status
- "Living off the land" attacks use existing system tools instead of bringing in new malware
- Attackers actively hide their tracks by disabling logs and clearing traces
- Traditional antivirus struggles against these techniques
- Behavioral analysis and EDR solutions offer better detection
- Multi-layer security approaches are essential

CHAPTER 8
ZERO-DAY ATTACKS — THE UNKNOWN THREAT

Imagine a door in your house that you don't know exists. You can't lock it because you don't know it's there. Meanwhile, a burglar has found it and walks in whenever they want.

That's a zero-day vulnerability.

Zero-day attacks exploit security flaws that nobody knows about — not the software company, not security researchers, not you. By the time anyone discovers the problem, the attackers have already been inside.

This chapter reveals why zero-day attacks are among the most dangerous threats organizations face — and why they're becoming increasingly common.

What Makes Zero-Day Different

Most cyberattacks exploit known vulnerabilities. A security researcher finds a flaw. The software company releases a patch. Organizations apply the patch. Problem solved.

Zero-day attacks break this cycle.

"A zero-day vulnerability is a type of security flaw that remains unknown to software developers and defenders, making it extremely dangerous, as attackers can exploit it without detection."

The timeline works in the attacker's favor:

1. Attacker discovers a flaw
2. Attacker develops an exploit
3. Attacker launches attacks
4. Eventually, someone notices
5. Software company develops a patch
6. Organizations deploy the patch

Between steps 1 and 6, attackers have free access. That window can last weeks, months, or even years.

One expert described the challenge:

"A zero-day vulnerability attack on supply chains is the most challenging endeavor, because there is no way to prevent a specific exploit before it occurs. The longer it remains undetected, the longer a cybercriminal can cause massive damage and keep spreading their payloads across the network to infect other network nodes."

Living in the Dark

The most alarming aspect of zero-day attacks is that victims often have no idea they've been compromised.

One expert shared:

"I never knew that a zero-day vulnerability existed in our network systems until the forensics team completed their work and reported back to us about the zero-day attack."

Another explained how long attackers can remain hidden:

"Zero-day attacks on the supply chain became more common these days, where attackers remain hidden in the systems for an extended time, often taking weeks or months before activating the actual attack."

During that hidden period, attackers can do significant damage:

"The danger of a zero-day attack is that it enables cyber actors to obtain higher access rights, download confidential data, and modify the system configuration while disguising themselves to remain undetected for an extended time."

Why Traditional Security Fails

Your antivirus software works by recognizing known threats. It has a database of malware signatures digital fingerprints of known bad software.

Zero-day attacks don't have signatures yet. They're unknown.

"Most automatic vulnerability scanning software compares suspicious code with signatures of known malware, and thus sometimes fails to detect new or unknown malware attacks such as zero-day attacks on the supply chain."

One expert put it bluntly:

"There are many reasons why detection software can fail to detect a ransomware infection, including adopting evasion tactics, using fileless attacks, and employing zero-day exploits; when combined together, antivirus cannot detect these ransomware attacks."

Another emphasized:

"Traditional signature-based antivirus programs or anti-malware systems cannot detect zero-day attacks on the supply chain."

The Supply Chain Problem

Zero-day attacks have found their perfect target: supply chains.

Modern businesses don't operate in isolation. They connect with suppliers, vendors, partners, and service providers. Each connection is a potential entry point.

One expert explained:

"Supply chain cyberattacks are successful because attackers exploit the trust relationship between business partners, including vendors, contractors, or service providers, allowing them to bypass traditional security defenses and gain access to an organization's computer systems, data, or infrastructure."

The complexity creates opportunity:

"Each link in the supply chain may have different security strengths and limitations, making it vulnerable to cyberattacks."

"A supplier may not have the same level of security posture as the primary company, creating a weak point in the supply chain that attackers can easily exploit."

How Supply Chain Attacks Work

The research revealed how these attacks unfold:

Step 1: Find the Weak Link

Attackers identify a vulnerable third party — a software vendor, service provider, or business partner with weaker security.

"An attacker first compromises a third-party supplier or business partner application or network and then elevates their privileges to steal data from a trusted business partner and spread the infection across another trusted network."

Step 2: Compromise Trusted Software

Attackers inject malicious code into legitimate software. This might be a software update, a development tool, or an open-source component.

"A year ago, I investigated supply chain attacks and found that cyber actors disguised their ransomware code in third-party software updates that were set to be downloaded automatically."

Step 3: Let Trust Do the Work

When organizations update their software — doing exactly what security best practices recommend — they install the malware themselves.

"These days, it is more frequent to see zero-day actors on the supply chain, where the attackers deliver their malicious software leveraging Windows application updates that allow for automatic downloads without human intervention."

Step 4: Spread Through the Network

Once inside one organization, attackers can potentially access every organization in that supply chain.

"A single compromise of a network node could have a domino effect on several businesses."

The Open-Source Risk

Open-source software powers much of the modern digital world. It's in operating systems, web servers, applications, and countless other tools.

But its openness creates risk:

"Although open-source code software enhances business operations and functions, cyber actors exploit open-source software vulnerabilities by concealing ransomware code to infiltrate the victim's machine or device."

"Vulnerabilities in open-source software, such as in Java-based applications, allow attackers to perform remote code execution on targeted network systems without authentication."

The Log4j vulnerability demonstrated this dramatically — a single flaw in a widely-used logging library affected millions of systems worldwide.

"The Log4j vulnerability, where a zero-day vulnerability in the Log4j software library was exploited by cybercriminals, allowed the attackers to remotely control devices running Java applications."

Small Companies, Big Targets

You might think zero-day attacks target only large corporations. The research says otherwise:

"Small-to medium-sized companies are most targeted by zero-day attacks on the supply chain, as they are more likely to operate using applications that lack updated security patches."

Smaller companies often:

- Have limited security budgets
- Use older, unpatched software
- Lack dedicated security staff
- Serve as entry points to larger partners

The Detection Dilemma

Zero-day attacks are challenging to detect by definition. But the research identified some approaches that help:

Behavioral Analysis

Instead of looking for known malware signatures, look for unusual behavior.

"Given the evasive nature of today's zero-day attacks, hybrid detection is the optimum method to detect and prevent zero-day attackers."

Network Segmentation

Limit the damage by limiting access:

"Network micro-segmentation is the most effective solution for preventing cyberattacks involving zero-day attacks on the supply chain from spreading to trusted partner network systems."

"Dividing a more extensive network into smaller subnets with less interconnectivity can help limit attackers from exploiting unpatched vulnerabilities and moving laterally across the network."

Continuous Monitoring

"A zero-day vulnerability in the supply chain becomes a real security challenge that requires continuous monitoring for early detection of the weakest link in the chain of trust."

"I always suggest for our clients to track and monitor business partners' activities on shared network systems to protect the interconnected supply chains."

Zero-Trust Architecture

Don't trust anyone or anything by default:

"Implementing a zero-trust policy and micro-segmentation of the network to limit access to critical data to only what is necessary for functionality significantly reduced the risk of zero-day vulnerability attacks."

The Legacy Software Problem

Old software is dangerous software. One expert shared a sobering discovery:

"Two years ago, I conducted a series of investigations on suspicious ransomware intrusion in our company's network systems. I found that the attacker had exploited a zero-day vulnerability in legacy software that had not been patched for two years."

The lesson: software that hasn't been updated in years may contain vulnerabilities that are now well-known to attackers, even if they were originally zero-days.

No Perfect Defense

The experts were honest about limitations:

"There is no standard security template procedure for detecting or preventing zero-day attacks on the supply chain."

"Zero-day vulnerability attacks are hazardous to business organizations because there are no defense mechanisms in place when they happen, offering a significant advantage for ransomware actors as they can exploit the flaw before the security vendor can release a patch."

But that doesn't mean organizations are helpless. Layered defenses, continuous monitoring, and rapid response capabilities all reduce risk and limit damage.

The Growing Threat

The research suggests zero-day attacks will become more common, not less:

"With the increasing interconnection of global supply chains, zero-day vulnerability attacks on supply chains continue to rise, making supply chains a significant security concern."

"Securing third-party software would be one of the future security challenges facing software supply chains."

What Comes Next

Zero-day attacks exploit unknown vulnerabilities. But there's another class of attack that's equally frightening: fileless ransomware.

In the next chapter, we'll explore how attackers operate entirely in memory, leaving no files on disk for security software to scan. These ghost-like attacks are among the hardest to detect — and they're becoming increasingly common.

Key Takeaways

- Zero-day attacks exploit vulnerabilities unknown to software developers and security teams
- Attackers can remain hidden for weeks or months before detection
- Traditional signature-based security tools cannot detect zero-day attacks
- Supply chains are prime targets because attackers can compromise multiple organizations through one weak link
- Open-source software creates particular risks due to its widespread use
- Small and medium businesses are frequently targeted
- Behavioral analysis and network segmentation offer better protection than signature-based detection
- Zero-trust architecture limits damage when breaches occur
- Legacy software with old, unpatched vulnerabilities is especially dangerous
- There is no perfect defense, but layered security reduces risk

CHAPTER 9
FILELESS RANSOMWARE — THE GHOST IN THE MACHINE

Traditional malware leaves footprints. It writes files to your hard drive. Security software can scan those files, identify them as malicious, and delete them.

Fileless ransomware doesn't play by those rules.

It lives entirely in memory. It uses your own Windows tools against you. It leaves no files behind for antivirus to scan. And when you restart your computer, it can come right back — still invisible.

This chapter reveals how these ghost-like attacks work and why they represent one of the most challenging threats organizations face.

What Makes Fileless Different

Traditional malware works like this:

1. Malicious file arrives (via email, download, etc.)
2. File is written to hard drive
3. File executes
4. Antivirus scans and (hopefully) detects it

Fileless ransomware breaks this pattern:

"Fileless ransomware attacks are persistent and difficult to eradicate because they embed malicious code in a computer's memory (RAM) without leaving any traces on the hard drive."

One expert explained the fundamental difference:

"Unlike traditional malware attacks that leave traces written to the filesystem on a local hard disk, fileless malware ideally leaves no trace after execution because it is a memory resident."

Another described the challenge:

"Fileless ransomware is incredibly challenging to detect because it operates directly from the computer's memory. Thus, it remains persistent for a long time and leaves no footprints on the local hard drive to investigate using traditional forensic tools."

Living Off the Land

Security researchers call these attacks "living off the land" because attackers use tools already present on the system rather than bringing their own.

One expert explained:

"Fileless attacks, better known as living-off-the-land attacks, are becoming more common among cybercriminals because they tend to be more effective than traditional malware attacks, as it is far more challenging to detect using legacy security tools such as traditional antivirus products that rely on signature-based prevention and detection methods."

Another described how it works:

"In a fileless attack, threat actors commonly leverage legitimate Windows built-in tools or stolen credentials to perform a range of malicious activities, including escalating privileges, accessing different systems and networks, stealing or encrypting data, delivering their payload, and setting a backdoor to advance their attack path."

The key insight:

"An attacker does not require the installation of malicious codes or scripts within the target system. Instead, cyber actors leverage native tools in the Windows environment, such as PowerShell or Task Scheduler, to automatically perform routine tasks on a chosen computer or network system."

PowerShell: The Attacker's Best Friend

PowerShell appears repeatedly in fileless attacks. It's pre-installed on every Windows system, it's incredibly powerful, and security tools trust it.

"PowerShell remains the primary tool for creating malicious scripts because security tools like antivirus or anti-malware programs view PowerShell as a trusted program within the Windows family."

Attackers use PowerShell for everything:

"Fileless ransomware avoids traditional file-based detection as it often leverages techniques like code injections to execute malicious code directly in Windows memory or uses a legitimate PowerShell script to steal credentials, elevate privileges, and encrypt files."

And they design their attacks specifically around it:

"Fileless ransomware designs scripts using PowerShell to evade detection."

The obfuscation techniques are sophisticated:

"The obfuscation techniques used by fileless ransomware are extremely challenging to detect using signature-based analysis, sandboxing, or even machine learning."

The Windows Registry Trick

Attackers don't just use memory — they also hide in the Windows Registry, which allows them to survive system reboots.

"More often, I investigated ransomware infections on Windows machines and found traces of fileless infections hidden in the Windows Registry, allowing the attackers to achieve persistence and perform lateral movement while remaining undetected."

One expert explained how this persistence works:

"I have seen attackers load a malicious DLL file into memory and registry hives for weeks or months before launching their malicious activity, regardless of system reboots, credential changes, or shutdowns."

Another noted:

"Fileless ransomware actors often tweak and manipulate Windows Registry features and configuration settings to maintain persistence and perform malicious tasks on a victim host or environment."

Exploit Kits and Automation

Attackers have automated these techniques using exploit kits:

"Cyber actors use exploit kits for large-scale fileless ransomware distribution without users' knowledge, requiring less time and effort than would be needed using traditional techniques."

This automation makes attacks more common and more dangerous.

Why Traditional Security Fails

Traditional antivirus looks for files. Fileless attacks don't use files.

"Signature-based prevention and detection methods cannot identify fileless attacks."

"Traditional security solutions are ineffective in entirely preventing or detecting fileless attacks."

One expert was blunt about the limitations:

"Fileless attacks are insidious and manipulative, making them more challenging. Thus, an attacker does not require the installation of malicious codes or scripts within the target system."

The problem is fundamental:

"Traditional ransomware detection analysis solutions cannot detect or block fileless attacks that exploit built-in Windows programs and applications, run in memory, and maintain persistence on the infected system or network."

Three Distinct Challenges

The research identified three core challenges that fileless ransomware poses:

Challenge 1: Trusted Tools

"Fileless ransomware exploits legitimate Windows system applications such as PowerShell to execute malicious commands, making it difficult to detect."

How do you block PowerShell when your IT team uses it every day?

Challenge 2: No Traces

"It runs its malicious code directly into Windows memory or hides it in the Windows registry, leaving no trace on the hard drive to detect."

No files means nothing to scan.

Challenge 3: Full Attack Capability

"Once inside the compromised system, fileless ransomware can perform a series of malicious activities, including lateral movement across a network, privilege escalation, data exfiltration, and deploying additional malicious payloads across the infected network system."

Fileless doesn't mean limited. These attacks can do everything traditional malware can do — and more.

Real Attack Examples

The experts shared what they've encountered:

Hidden in Plain Sight

"In our company, we have a few machines that have been infected with some kind of fileless malware using PowerShell commands and scheduled task services that run DLL malicious code."

Persistence Through Reboots

"I witnessed fileless ransomware actors exploiting legitimate Windows tools, like Microsoft Office macros, PowerShell script, and compressed zip file, to carry out malicious activities, making detection and remediation a daunting task."

Detection Indicators

"Whenever I see unauthorized use of PowerShell commands or a scheduled task running on startup, I conclude that an active fileless attack is in progress."

Hiding in Documents

Fileless attacks often start with familiar file types:

"Fileless ransomware actors evade detection by embedding malicious code into Microsoft Word and other file formats such as PDF files, zip files, or image files."

When you open a document with malicious macros, the attack runs in memory — no separate malware file needed.

Detection Strategies

The experts offered practical guidance on detecting these elusive attacks:

Behavioral Analysis

"Machine-learning-based behavioral analytics is an ideal tool when it comes to paying close attention to the signs of privilege escalation, unauthorized use of PowerShell, unfamiliar processes running in the main memory, or suspicious modifications performed in the Windows registry. These are the areas for detecting fileless-related activities that have evaded detection."

Know Your Environment

"Data security analysts must intimately understand their environment and be able to identify and differentiate between the legitimate use of Windows built-in tools such as PowerShell,

Windows memory, and registry, or exploit kits, which are misused by fileless ransomware attacks."

Monitor PowerShell

"The first thing to look for is the signs of the unauthorized usage of PowerShell scripts on the system."

Analyze Memory and Registry

"By analyzing memory and Windows Registry, we got a lot of intelligent artifacts of fileless ransomware indicating fileless persistent behavior in the system."

Vulnerability Scanning

"Run vulnerability scanning manually to identify vulnerabilities in applications such as Microsoft Office, PDF, or ZIP files."

Prevention Measures

Beyond detection, the experts recommended proactive steps:

Disable Unnecessary Features

"Blocking macros in Microsoft Word, as well as disabling the ability of PDFs to load in browsers, can minimize the chance of being a victim of a fileless attack."

"Disabling macros in MS Office is an excellent idea to eliminate hidden fileless code used to compromise a victim's system without relying on file-based delivery."

But Be Careful What You Disable

Some experts warned against being too aggressive:

"Disabling the PowerShell command hinders the defensive capabilities that PowerShell can provide, including helping with forensics investigation, incident response, and automating desktop tasks."

"Removing or restricting the PowerShell command would prevent administrators and defenders from utilizing PowerShell to assist with system maintenance, forensic work, and automation of security tasks."

The solution is monitoring and control, not outright elimination.

Behavioral Baselines

"I recommend utilizing behavior-detection analytics such as machine learning-enabled tools to track, analyze, and interpret user interaction data on digital platforms and identify fileless-triggered activities that deviate from a baseline."

The Backup Problem

Fileless ransomware creates a particular challenge for backup strategies:

"Any business organization that relies on backups alone as data recovery strategy will face many challenges when it comes to recovering ransomware encrypted data, especially against fileless ransomware attacks or zero-day attacks."

And:

"This technique renders the backup ineffective for recovering the data."

Backups remain important, but they're not a complete solution against these sophisticated attacks.

A Multi-Layer Approach

The consensus among experts was clear: no single solution works.

"The key to a successful detection approach against fileless ransomware is an integrated multilayered approach that addresses the entire ransomware threat lifecycle."

This should include:

- Behavioral analysis and monitoring
- Endpoint Detection and Response (EDR) solutions
- Memory and registry analysis capabilities
- User activity baselines
- Controlled use of PowerShell and macros
- Regular security updates
- Employee training on document-based attacks

"Although security vendors continue to improve their detection and prevention capabilities for file-based attacks, cybercriminals adapt and develop new techniques, such as fileless ransomware or zero-day attacks, to infect the victim's machine and quickly spread laterally to other machines to cause additional damage."

This Ends Part III

We've now covered the security holes attackers exploit:

- Windows exploitation through DLL injection and PowerShell (Chapter 7)

- Zero-day attacks on unknown vulnerabilities (Chapter 8)
- Fileless ransomware that lives in memory (Chapter 9)

In Part IV, we'll look at the bigger picture: why ransomware keeps growing despite all our defenses. We'll explore the role of Ransomware-as-a-Service, cryptocurrency, and artificial intelligence in fueling this epidemic — and what the future might hold.

Key Takeaways

- Fileless ransomware operates in memory without writing files to disk
- "Living off the land" attacks use legitimate Windows tools like PowerShell
- Traditional antivirus cannot detect fileless attacks because there are no files to scan
- Attackers persist through reboots by hiding in the Windows Registry
- PowerShell is the #1 tool for fileless attacks due to its power and trusted status
- Detection requires behavioral analysis, not signature-based scanning
- Monitor for unusual PowerShell activity, registry changes, and memory processes
- Disabling macros in Office documents reduces risk
- Backups alone are insufficient against fileless ransomware

- A multi-layer security approach is essential

PART IV

WHY ATTACKS KEEP GROWING

CHAPTER 10
THE PERFECT STORM

Despite billions spent on cybersecurity, ransomware attacks keep increasing. Despite arrests, takedowns, and sanctions, new criminal groups keep appearing. Despite all our warnings and training, organizations keep getting hit.

Why?

Because ransomware has become the perfect crime. Multiple factors have converged to create an environment where attacks are easy to launch, hard to stop, and incredibly profitable.

This chapter examines the forces driving the ransomware epidemic — and what the future holds.

The Money Motive

At its core, ransomware is about money. Everything else flows from this simple fact.

"Making money is the primary reason behind the recent surge in ransomware attacks against various business organizations; because it is the easiest way for cyber actors to make money by subscribing for RaaS service, while sitting behind a keyboard."

The economics are compelling. Attackers can:

- Launch attacks remotely from anywhere in the world
- Target multiple victims simultaneously
- Demand payments ranging from thousands to millions of dollars

- Remain largely anonymous
- Face minimal risk of prosecution

One expert captured it vividly:

"Imagine if people were able to steal data, walk away, and threaten the company to pay us a huge ransom without getting caught. This is the way cybercriminals get paid on the dark web."

Cryptocurrency: The Enabler

Before Bitcoin, collecting ransom was the hard part. How do you get paid without revealing your identity? Bank transfers leave trails. Cash requires physical handoffs.

Cryptocurrency solved this problem.

"Bitcoin became the de facto standard currency for ransom payments."

"Cryptocurrency is the preferred payment method, making it harder for data security professionals to trace or identify the recipients of ransom payments."

The advantages for criminals are significant:

"Bitcoin payments are advantageous for cybercriminals, as they allow for the movement of ransom money while masking their identity, complicating investigative efforts for defenders."

"Cybercriminals often exploit untraceable methods such as cryptocurrency to collect ransoms, making it exceedingly difficult to track or recover funds once they have been paid."

Without cryptocurrency, modern ransomware as we know it couldn't exist.

The RaaS Revolution

We covered Ransomware-as-a-Service in Chapter 3, but its impact on the epidemic deserves emphasis here.

RaaS didn't just make attacks easier. It industrialized cybercrime.

"The RaaS business model has become increasingly popular among cybercriminals, making it easier for RaaS affiliates with limited technical skills to launch successful ransomware attacks."

"RaaS helps lower the barrier to entry for cybercriminals and expands their attack surface, making it more difficult for business organizations to combat ransomware threats effectively."

The result: more attackers, more attacks, more victims.

"Ransomware attacks continue to increase in frequency and sophistication owing to the collaboration among specialized cybercriminal groups, leveraging the RaaS business platform, making it easier to sell ready-to-operate ransomware toolkits and auction the stolen data to the highest bidder on the dark web."

Double Extortion: Raising the Stakes

Traditional ransomware gave victims a choice: pay or lose your data.

Double extortion removes that choice for many organizations.

"Data exfiltration and double extortion tactics have become standard tactics for modern ransomware attacks, where profits obtained through data exfiltration and the digital extortion of victims have become significant factors motivating cybercriminals to develop more adaptive and stealthy ransomware codes."

Even organizations with perfect backups face pressure:

"In the past, a victimized business organization could leverage backups to restore compromised data. However, by adopting the tactics of data exfiltration out of the network and threatening to publish stolen data in public, modern cyber actors added additional pressure on victims to pay for data recovery."

The psychological impact is significant:

"Data exfiltration and double extortion take ransomware threats a step further by adding a layer of psychological and financial pressure to the victim."

The Adaptability Factor

What makes ransomware groups so dangerous is their ability to adapt.

"Ransomware groups have demonstrated remarkable adaptability, swiftly changing tactics and techniques in response to traditional defense mechanisms, such as antivirus solutions. This adaptability underscored the critical need for business organizations to remain vigilant and proactively adjust their security measures."

When defenders develop new protections, attackers develop new bypasses. When one attack vector gets blocked, they find another.

"Ransomware threat actors continued to develop complex and sophisticated ransomware variants, including Crypto-Ransomware, Locker-Ransomware, and Extortion-Ransomware. These ransomware variants pose significant dangers to business organizations due to their increasingly complex tactics and techniques."

The AI Arms Race

Artificial intelligence is changing both sides of the fight. And right now, attackers are gaining ground.

AI-Powered Attacks

"Modern cybercriminals increasingly leverage emerging advanced technologies such as Artificial Intelligence and Machine Learning to enhance their attacks, making them more sophisticated, targeted, and difficult to detect."

"Modern ransomware actors utilize these technologies to automate tasks, customize attacks, evade detection, and increase their success rates in stealing data."

The applications are alarming:

"With AI-powered ransomware, attackers can create more tailored and creative emails that prompt victims to click on a link, triggering autonomous downloads of malicious code onto their machines or devices."

"With AI, cyber actors can create more personalized and authentic-looking phishing emails that are harder to detect."

Even deepfakes are being weaponized:

"Cyber actors can leverage AI-empowered tools to create fake videos that mimic marketing departments and send them to recipients via email, prompting victims to respond to a special offer or register for a webinar, which may lead to a ransomware attack."

AI-Powered Defense

Defenders are also using AI, with some success:

"A hybrid-based detection analysis, powered by a subset of Artificial Intelligence algorithms, such as Machine Learning and Deep Learning, is the most common approach for detecting and preventing modern ransomware attacks at an early stage."

But there are limitations:

"The effectiveness of AI-enabled models depends on well-trained and updated datasets for analysis to detect and prevent unknown ransomware threats."

"AI-driven cybersecurity solutions also face challenges and drawbacks. Studies have shown that cybercriminals exploit AI to bolster their cyber operations, distribute malicious codes, and conceal their identities."

The Supply Chain Vulnerability

As businesses become more interconnected, they become more vulnerable.

"With the increasing interconnection of global supply chains, zero-day vulnerability attacks on supply chains continue to rise, making supply chains a significant security concern."

Attackers have recognized this opportunity:

"Cybercriminals increasingly target supply chains because they represent significant vulnerability and can provide access to a trusted network of multiple business organizations."

"By compromising these network-trusted entities, ransomware actors can gain a foothold in the supply chain ecosystem and potentially access the company's network resources for an extended period of time."

One breach can cascade through an entire ecosystem.

The Remote Work Factor

The shift to remote work during the pandemic expanded attack surfaces dramatically.

"With the increased adoption of remote work environments, cybercriminals shifted to the RaaS business, which is a relatively low-risk business, providing an opportunity for attackers to make money easily by extorting victims."

Organizations that hastily deployed VPNs and remote access solutions often left security gaps. Many of those gaps remain.

The Cloud Frontier

As organizations move data to the cloud, attackers follow.

"In the future, cyber threats will focus more on data exfiltration than on historical data encryption."

"There will likely be an increase in cloud-based ransomware attacks as many companies continue to move their critical data into cloud storage environments."

Cloud environments offer new opportunities for attackers — and new challenges for defenders.

What the Experts Predict

The security experts offered sobering predictions about the future:

More Automation

"In the far future, businesses will encounter an increase in ransomware proliferation through automation, leveraging AI capabilities to conduct faster and more stealthy attacks against victims."

"Cybercriminals will shift their focus toward automation to create and send personalized malicious email messages and SMS messages."

Smarter AI Attacks

"Ransomware actors will leverage the power of artificial intelligence to automate distributed denial of service (DDoS) attacks against multiple devices connected online or flood network systems with false alerts."

"Using machine learning algorithms, ransomware can transform and disguise itself in scripts to evade detection and scan the network, making it more challenging to detect and eliminate."

Continued RaaS Growth

"In the future, the RaaS business model will gain more traction among cybercriminals by monetizing stolen data, extorting victims, and threatening to leak data to the public if the ransom is not paid."

Supply Chain Targeting

"Ransomware tactics will continue to evolve and become more sophisticated, targeting various business organizations, including suppliers, vendors, and third-party service providers."

"With the increasing interconnectedness of the global supply chain ecosystem, ransomware attacks targeting supply chain partners are expected to rise."

AI-Enabled Exploit Kits

"Cybercriminals will continue to thrive by selling and leasing AI ransomware exploit kit capabilities to their loyal affiliates, causing large-scale damage to their target businesses."

The Defense Imperative

Despite these challenges, the experts didn't counsel despair. They emphasized that organizations can protect themselves — if they take the threat seriously.

"Ransomware threats will continue to evolve in response to corporate defensive strategies, law enforcement successes, and government sanctions."

The key is a comprehensive, multi-layered approach:

"A comprehensive multi-layered security approach is essential for preventing and detecting evasive ransomware threats."

This includes:

- Prevention (training, patching, access controls)

- Detection (behavioral analysis, monitoring, AI-powered tools)
- Response (incident plans, backup strategies)
- Recovery (tested restoration procedures)

The Regulatory Response

The experts predicted increased regulatory pressure:

"Zero-day vulnerability attacks on supply chains would pressure cybersecurity regulators and policymakers to enact policies demanding that business organizations operate using a more secure and trusted supply chain ecosystem."

Government action — sanctions, law enforcement cooperation, and mandatory security standards — will play an increasing role in the fight against ransomware.

The Bigger Picture

Ransomware isn't going away. The economic incentives are too strong. The barriers to entry are too low. The risks for attackers are too small.

But understanding why attacks keep growing is the first step to mounting an effective defense. Organizations that recognize the forces at work — the RaaS model, cryptocurrency, AI, supply chain vulnerabilities — can build protections specifically designed to counter them.

The experts in this research made one thing clear: the organizations that will survive are those that take ransomware seriously, invest in comprehensive security, and never stop adapting.

Because the attackers never stop adapting either.

Key Takeaways

- Financial motivation drives the ransomware epidemic — it's the easiest way for criminals to make money
- Cryptocurrency enabled modern ransomware by solving the payment problem
- RaaS industrialized cybercrime, allowing anyone to launch attacks
- Double extortion removes the backup escape route for many organizations
- AI is being weaponized by attackers to create more convincing and evasive attacks
- Supply chain interconnection creates cascading vulnerabilities
- Remote work expanded attack surfaces that remain vulnerable
- Cloud environments are the next frontier for ransomware attacks
- Attacks will become more automated, AI-powered, and targeted
- Multi-layer security approaches are essential for defense
- Regulatory pressure will increase
- Organizations that take the threat seriously and continuously adapt will survive

CONCLUSION: DEFENDING THE FUTURE

We began this book with a simple question: why do ransomware attacks keep succeeding despite everything we've learned about them?

The answer, as we've discovered, is both simple and complex.

Simple: because ransomware works. It's profitable, relatively low-risk for attackers, and exploits fundamental weaknesses in how organizations operate.

Complex: because the ransomware ecosystem has evolved into a sophisticated industry with specialized roles, professional services, and continuous innovation. Defending against it requires understanding not just the technology, but the economics, psychology, and organizational factors that make attacks successful.

What We've Learned

This book drew on research with seventeen security experts who have spent years on the front lines of ransomware defense. Their experiences reveal several critical insights:

Ransomware has fundamentally changed. It's no longer just about encrypting files. Modern attacks involve data theft, double extortion, and sophisticated evasion techniques. Attackers steal your data before encrypting it, then threaten to publish it if you don't pay — even if you have backups.

The attack surface keeps expanding. Phishing emails remain the primary vector, but attackers also exploit malicious websites, vulnerable remote access systems, zero-day vulnerabilities, and supply chain weaknesses. Every connection point is a potential entry.

Attackers use your own tools against you. DLL injection, PowerShell abuse, and fileless techniques allow attackers to operate using legitimate Windows features. Traditional antivirus struggles to detect activity that looks like normal system operations.

The RaaS model industrialized cybercrime. Ransomware-as-a-Service lowered barriers to entry, enabling anyone to launch attacks. Cryptocurrency solved the payment problem. Together, they created an epidemic.

AI is changing the battlefield. Attackers use artificial intelligence to create more convincing phishing campaigns, automate attacks, and evade detection. Defenders use AI for behavioral analysis and threat detection. The arms race continues.

No single solution works. Every expert emphasized this point: defending against modern ransomware requires multiple layers of protection working together.

The Multi-Layer Imperative

If there's one message that echoes throughout this research, it's this:

"A multi-layered security defense mechanism is crucial in detecting and preventing ransomware threats and reducing the risk of successful cyberattacks."

What does multi-layer defense look like in practice?

Prevention Layer

- Employee training and awareness programs
- Email filtering and web security

- Access controls and least-privilege principles
- Regular patching and updates
- Network segmentation
- Zero-trust architecture

Detection Layer

- Behavioral analysis and anomaly detection
- Endpoint Detection and Response (EDR)
- Security Information and Event Management (SIEM)
- Continuous monitoring
- Deception technologies (honeypots, honeytokens)

Response Layer

- Incident response plans
- Forensic capabilities
- Communication protocols
- Legal and regulatory compliance procedures

Recovery Layer

- Tested backup and restoration procedures
- Business continuity plans
- Disaster recovery capabilities

No single layer is sufficient. Attackers who bypass one layer should encounter another. The goal isn't to make attacks impossible — it's to make them difficult, detectable, and recoverable.

The Human Factor

Technology alone cannot solve the ransomware problem. The experts were unanimous: people remain both the greatest vulnerability and the greatest defense.

"Providing security awareness training programs for employees is paramount for business organizations to proactively protect their data, mitigate ransomware risks, and foster a culture of best security practices."

Effective training isn't a once-a-year checkbox exercise. It's ongoing, practical, and tailored to the actual threats employees face. It includes:

- Recognizing phishing attempts
- Safe browsing practices
- Incident reporting procedures
- Understanding the stakes

When employees become active participants in security rather than passive targets, the entire organization becomes more resilient.

The Collaboration Imperative

Ransomware isn't just an individual organization's problem. It's a systemic threat that requires systemic responses.

"Defense against modern ransomware threats requires coordinated efforts by many data-security stakeholders."

This means:

- **Information sharing** between organizations about threats and tactics
- **Public-private partnerships** between businesses and law enforcement
- **Industry collaboration** on standards and best practices
- **Supply chain security** with vendors and partners
- **Regulatory frameworks** that establish baseline requirements

No organization is an island. The interconnected nature of modern business means that one company's vulnerability can become another's crisis. Collaboration isn't optional — it's essential.

The Ethical Dimension

One question haunts every ransomware victim: should we pay?

The experts in this research strongly advised against it:

- Payment doesn't guarantee data recovery
- It funds and encourages future attacks
- It may violate sanctions laws
- It marks you as a willing payer for future targeting

Yet the decision isn't always clear-cut. When patient data is at stake, when critical infrastructure is down, when jobs hang in the balance the theoretical becomes painfully practical.

The best solution is to never face that choice. Invest in prevention. Prepare for recovery. Make paying unnecessary.

Looking Forward

The ransomware threat isn't going away. The experts predict:

- **More AI-powered attacks** — sophisticated, personalized, and harder to detect
- **Increased supply chain targeting** — hitting multiple organizations through shared vulnerabilities
- **Continued RaaS growth** — further lowering barriers to entry
- **Cloud-focused attacks** — following data to new environments
- **Greater automation** — scaling attacks to unprecedented levels

But they also predict stronger defenses, increased regulation, and growing collaboration. The battle isn't lost — it's ongoing.

A Final Word

Writing this book required confronting uncomfortable truths. Ransomware succeeds because:

- We don't patch quickly enough
- We use weak passwords
- We click links we shouldn't
- We trust when we should verify
- We prioritize convenience over security
- We assume it won't happen to us

These aren't just technical failures. They're human failures. Organizational failures. Cultural failures.

Fixing them requires more than buying new security tools. It requires changing how we think about risk, how we invest in protection, and how we prepare for the worst.

The seventeen experts who contributed to this research have seen ransomware's damage firsthand. They've helped organizations recover from devastating attacks. They've watched businesses fail and data disappear forever.

Their message is clear: the threat is real, it's growing, and it requires serious attention.

But their message is also hopeful: organizations that take ransomware seriously, that invest in comprehensive defenses, that train their people and prepare for incidents — these organizations survive. They recover. They become stronger.

The choice is yours.

Key Recommendations

Based on everything covered in this book, here are the essential actions every organization should take:

Immediately

1. Enable multi-factor authentication everywhere
2. Review and restrict remote access configurations
3. Ensure backups are tested, ofline, and protected
4. Establish an incident response plan

Short-term

5. Implement employee security awareness training

6. Deploy endpoint detection and response solutions

7. Segment your network to limit lateral movement

8. Patch systems promptly, prioritizing internet-facing applications

Ongoing

9. Adopt a zero-trust security model

10. Monitor for unusual behavior, not just known threats

11. Conduct regular security assessments and penetration tests

12. Stay informed about emerging threats and tactics

13. Collaborate with industry peers and law enforcement

14. Review and update your security posture continuously

The ransomware threat will continue to evolve. Your defenses must evolve with it.

Thank you for reading. Stay safe. Stay vigilant. Stay prepared.

APPENDIX

ABOUT THE RESEARCH

This book is based on a doctoral dissertation conducted at the University of the Cumberlands, examining the evolving tactics and techniques of modern ransomware threats to business organizations. The research employed a qualitative phenomenological methodology to understand the lived experiences of data security experts who deal with ransomware incidents in their professional roles.

The Experts

Seventeen data security professionals participated in this study. They were selected based on specific criteria:

- Minimum of two years of experience in information security
- Direct experience dealing with ransomware threats
- Employment in U.S.-based business organizations
- Roles including security analysts, IT managers, incident responders, network engineers, and cybersecurity specialists

The participants' experience ranged from five to 20 years in cybersecurity, providing a wealth of practical knowledge about ransomware attacks, defense strategies, and organizational responses.

Research Method

Data Collection

Participants were interviewed using semi-structured, open-ended questions designed to explore their experiences with ransomware threats. Each interview lasted approximately 45-60 minutes and was conducted via video conference. All interviews were recorded and transcribed verbatim.

The interview questions addressed seven core areas:

1. Lived experiences dealing with ransomware threats
2. Common attack vectors
3. Prevention solutions
4. Detection methods
5. Factors enabling the rise of ransomware
6. Consequences of paying or not paying ransom
7. Future ransomware landscape

Data Analysis

The transcribed interviews were analyzed using inductive thematic analysis, a method that allows themes to emerge naturally from the data rather than being imposed by predetermined categories. The analysis software NVivo was used to organize, code, and identify patterns across the dataset.

This process identified eight major themes and twelve subthemes that form the foundation of this book's content.

Research Quality

Several measures ensured the reliability and validity of the findings:

- **Member checking**: Participants reviewed their transcripts to verify accuracy
- **Triangulation**: Multiple data sources and perspectives were compared
- **Audit trail**: Every step of the research process was documented
- **Bracketing**: The researcher set aside preconceptions to allow participants' experiences to speak for themselves
- **Saturation**: Data collection continued until no new themes emerged

Limitations

As with any research study, this work has limitations:

- The sample was limited to U.S.-based organizations
- Participants were purposefully selected, which may introduce selection bias
- The qualitative nature of the study means findings describe depth of experience rather than statistical prevalence
- The rapidly evolving nature of ransomware means some specific tactics may have changed since the research was conducted

Despite these limitations, the themes and insights that emerged provide valuable guidance for understanding and defending against ransomware threats.

Adaptation for This Book

The original dissertation followed academic conventions and contained extensive literature reviews, methodology discussions, and theoretical frameworks. For this book, the research findings have been reorganized and rewritten to be accessible to business professionals and IT practitioners while maintaining fidelity to the original expert insights.

Direct quotes from participants appear throughout the book, identified by participant codes (P1 through P17) in the original research. These quotes have been lightly edited for clarity while preserving their meaning and the experts' voices.

GLOSSARY

Advanced Persistent Threat (APT) A prolonged and targeted cyberattack in which an intruder gains access to a network and remains undetected for an extended period, often to steal data rather than cause immediate damage.

Affiliate In the context of Ransomware-as-a-Service, an individual or group that rents or purchases ransomware tools from developers and uses them to conduct attacks, sharing profits with the developers.

Backup A copy of data stored separately from the original, used to restore information in case of data loss. Effective ransomware defense requires backups that are tested, ofline, and protected from encryption.

Behavioral Analysis A security approach that detects threats by monitoring for unusual patterns of activity rather than relying on known malware signatures.

Bitcoin A cryptocurrency commonly used for ransomware payments due to its perceived anonymity and ease of cross-border transfer.

Brute Force Attack A trial-and-error method of attempting to guess passwords or encryption keys by systematically trying all possible combinations.

Command and Control (C2) Server A computer controlled by attackers that is used to send commands to compromised systems and receive stolen data.

Cryptocurrency Digital currency that uses cryptography for security and operates on decentralized networks, making transactions difficult to trace.

Crypto-Ransomware Ransomware that encrypts files on a victim's system, making them inaccessible until a ransom is paid for the decryption key.

Dark Web The portion of the internet that is not indexed by search engines and requires special software (like Tor) to access, often used for illegal activities including ransomware operations.

Data Exfiltration The unauthorized transfer of data from a computer or network, often preceding ransomware encryption in double extortion attacks.

DLL (Dynamic Link Library) A file containing code and data that can be used by multiple programs simultaneously in Windows. Attackers exploit DLLs to inject malicious code into legitimate processes.

DLL Injection A technique where attackers insert malicious code into a running process by loading a malicious DLL, allowing them to execute code while appearing as a legitimate application.

Double Extortion A ransomware tactic where attackers both encrypt data and steal it, threatening to publish stolen information if the ransom isn't paid, even if the victim has backups.

Drive-by Download An unintentional download of malicious software that occurs simply by visiting a compromised website, without requiring user action.

EDR (Endpoint Detection and Response) Security software that monitors endpoints (computers, servers, mobile devices) for suspicious activity and provides tools to investigate and respond to threats.

Encryption The process of converting data into a coded format that can only be read with the correct decryption key.

Exploit Code that takes advantage of a vulnerability in software or hardware to cause unintended behavior, often to gain unauthorized access.

Exploit Kit A toolkit used by attackers to automatically identify and exploit vulnerabilities in systems, often delivered through compromised websites.

Fileless Malware/Ransomware Malicious software that operates entirely in memory without writing files to disk, making it difficult to detect with traditional antivirus tools.

Honeypot A decoy system designed to attract attackers and detect, deflect, or study hacking attempts.

Incident Response The organized approach to addressing and managing the aftermath of a security breach or cyberattack.

Lateral Movement The techniques attackers use to move through a network after gaining initial access, seeking valuable data and additional systems to compromise.

Living Off the Land An attack technique where adversaries use legitimate tools already present on a system (like PowerShell) rather than bringing in new malware, making detection more difficult.

Locker Ransomware Ransomware that locks users out of their devices entirely, rather than encrypting specific files.

Malvertising The use of online advertising to spread malware, often by placing malicious ads on legitimate websites.

Malware Any software intentionally designed to cause damage to a computer, server, network, or user.

Micro-segmentation A security technique that divides a network into small, isolated segments to limit lateral movement if a breach occurs.

Multi-Factor Authentication (MFA) A security method requiring users to provide two or more verification factors to access a resource, significantly reducing the risk of compromised credentials.

Obfuscation Techniques used to make code or data difficult to understand, often used by attackers to evade detection.

Payload The component of malware that performs the malicious action, such as encrypting files or stealing data.

Persistence Techniques attackers use to maintain access to a compromised system even after reboots or credential changes.

Phishing A social engineering attack that uses deceptive emails, websites, or messages to trick victims into revealing sensitive information or installing malware.

Phishing Kit A package of tools and templates that allows attackers to easily create convincing phishing campaigns.

Polymorphic Malware Malware that changes its code or signature with each infection, making it difficult to detect with signature-based tools.

PowerShell A powerful Windows scripting language and command-line shell frequently abused by attackers for executing malicious commands.

Privilege Escalation The exploitation of a vulnerability to gain elevated access to resources that are normally protected.

RaaS (Ransomware-as-a-Service) A business model where ransomware developers sell or lease their malware to other criminals (affiliates) who conduct attacks and share the profits.

Ransom Note The message displayed to ransomware victims explaining that their files have been encrypted and providing instructions for payment.

RDP (Remote Desktop Protocol) A Microsoft protocol that allows users to connect to and control a computer remotely, frequently targeted by ransomware attackers.

Sandbox An isolated testing environment used to analyze suspicious files or code without risking the broader system.

SIEM (Security Information and Event Management) Technology that provides real-time analysis of security alerts generated by applications and network hardware.

Signature-based Detection A security approach that identifies threats by comparing files or activities against a database of known malware signatures.

Social Engineering Psychological manipulation techniques used to trick people into making security mistakes or giving away sensitive information.

Spear Phishing A targeted phishing attack directed at a specific individual or organization, often using personalized information to appear more convincing.

Steganography The practice of hiding data within other files (like images) to avoid detection.

Supply Chain Attack An attack that targets an organization by compromising a trusted third party, such as a software vendor or business partner.

Task Scheduler A Windows component that allows users to schedule programs and scripts to run at specific times, often abused by attackers for persistence.

VPN (Virtual Private Network) Technology that creates an encrypted connection over the internet, commonly used for secure remote access but also a target for attackers.

Vulnerability A weakness in software, hardware, or processes that can be exploited by attackers.

Windows Registry A database in Windows that stores configuration settings, often targeted by attackers for persistence and to hide malicious code.

Zero-Day Vulnerability A security flaw unknown to the software vendor or security community, giving attackers an advantage because no patch exists.

Zero-Trust Architecture A security model that requires strict verification for every person and device trying to access resources, regardless of whether they are inside or outside the network perimeter.

RESOURCES

Government and Industry Resources

Cybersecurity and Infrastructure Security Agency (CISA) https://www.cisa.gov/stopransomware The U.S. government's primary resource for ransomware prevention, including alerts, guidance, and tools.

FBI Internet Crime Complaint Center (IC3) https://www.ic3.gov For reporting ransomware incidents and accessing threat information.

National Institute of Standards and Technology (NIST) https://www.nist.gov/cyberframework The NIST Cybersecurity Framework provides guidelines for managing and reducing cybersecurity risk.

No More Ransom Project https://www.nomoreransom.org A public-private initiative that provides free decryption tools for some ransomware variants.

MITRE ATT&CK Framework https://attack.mitre.org A comprehensive knowledge base of adversary tactics and techniques based on real-world observations.

Training and Awareness

SANS Institute https://www.sans.org Offers cybersecurity training, certifications, and resources including free security awareness materials.

KnowBe4 https://www.knowbe4.com Provides security awareness training and simulated phishing platforms.

Cybrary https://www.cybrary.it Offers free and paid cybersecurity training courses.

Threat Intelligence

VirusTotal https://www.virustotal.com Free service for analyzing suspicious files and URLs.

AlienVault Open Threat Exchange https://otx.alienvault.com Open threat intelligence community sharing indicators of compromise.

Recorded Future https://www.recordedfuture.com Threat intelligence platform with ransomware-specific research and reporting.

Incident Response

Incident Response Plan Templates CISA and NIST provide templates and guidelines for developing incident response plans.

Ransomware Response Checklist (CISA) https://www.cisa.gov/stopransomware/ransomware-guide Step-by-step guidance for responding to ransomware incidents.

Industry Reports and Research

Verizon Data Breach Investigations Report Annual report analyzing thousands of security incidents and data breaches.

IBM Cost of a Data Breach Report Annual study examining the financial impact of data breaches.

Sophos State of Ransomware Report Annual survey of ransomware trends and organizational responses.

Coveware Quarterly Ransomware Reports Detailed analysis of ransomware trends, payment amounts, and attack vectors.

Professional Organizations

Information Systems Security Association (ISSA) https://www.issa.org Global organization of information security professionals.

InfraGard https://www.infragard.org Partnership between the FBI and private sector focused on critical infrastructure protection.

Information Sharing and Analysis Centers (ISACs) Sector-specific organizations that share threat intelligence among members.

Books for Further Reading

Sandworm by Andy Greenberg — An in-depth look at state-sponsored cyberattacks and the NotPetya attack.

The Art of Intrusion by Kevin Mitnick — Stories of real-world hacking and social engineering.

Countdown to Zero Day by Kim Zetter — The story of Stuxnet and the evolution of cyber warfare.

This Is How They Tell Me the World Ends by Nicole Perlroth — An examination of the zero-day vulnerability market.

Staying Current

The ransomware landscape changes rapidly. Consider subscribing to:

- CISA alerts and advisories

- Security vendor blogs (Mandiant, CrowdStrike, Sophos, Palo Alto Networks)
- Security news sites (Krebs on Security, Bleeping Computer, The Hacker News)
- Industry newsletters and podcasts

ABOUT THE AUTHOR

Dr. Ahmed Tawer conducted the original research upon which this book is based as part of his doctoral studies at the University of the Cumberlands. His research focused on understanding the evolving tactics and techniques of modern ransomware threats through the lived experiences of data security experts.

Made in the USA
Monee, IL
05 November 2026

67914357R00080